In The Wild

Bears

Claire Robinson

© 1997 Reed Educational & Professional Publishing
Published by Heinemann Interactive Library,
an imprint of Reed Educational & Professional Publishing,
500 Coventry Lane.
Crystal Lake, IL 60014

Produced by Times, Malaysia
Designed by Celia Floyd
Cover design by Lucy Smith

01 00 99 98 97

10 9 8 7 6 5 4 3 2 1

ISBN 1-57572-134-1

Library of Congress Cataloging-in-Publication Data

Robinson, Claire, 1955-
    Bears / Claire Robinson.
      p. cm. -- (In the wild)
    Includes bibliographical references (p.   ) and index.
    Summary: Provides information about brown bears, especially those
living in Canada and Alaska, covering such topics as habitat,
finding food, mating, hibernation, raising cubs, and more.
    ISBN 1-57572-134-1 (lib. bdg.)
    1. Brown Bear--Alaska--Juvenile literature.   [1. Brown Bear.
2. Bears.]   I. Title. II. Series: Robinson, Claire, 1955-   In the
wild.
QL737.C27R58 1997
599. 784' 09798--dc21   97-1230 1
                                              CIP
                                              AC

Acknowledgements

The author and publishers are grateful to the following for permission to reproduce copyright photographs:
Oxford Scientific Films: Matthias Breiter, p.7; Daniel J Cox, pp.9, 16; David C Fritts, pp.15, 20;
Djuro Huber, p.17; Frank Huber, pp.4 (left), 12; G C Kelley, p.21; Jeff Lepore, p.13;
Zig Leszczynski, p.4 (right); C.C. Lockwood, p.8; James McCann, p.11; Joe McDonald, p.5 (left);
Tom Mettugh, p.10; Meyers, p.6; Norbert Rosing, p.5 (right); Leonard Lee Rue, p.18;
Frank Schneidermeyer, p.22; Stouffer Productions, p.19; Ronald Toms, p.23; Jim Zipp, p.14.

Cover photograph: Oxford Scientific Films

Special thanks to Oxford Scientific Films

Every effort has been made to contact copyright holders of any material reproduced in this book. Any omissions will be rectified in subsequent printings if notice is given to the publisher.

Some words are shown in bold, **like this**. You can find out what they mean by looking in the glossary.

Contents

Bear Relatives

Bears are some of the world's biggest **mammals**. There are seven different kinds of bears. Here you can see some of them.

brown bear

sloth bear

sun bear

polar bear

Polar bears are the largest bears. Sun bears are the smallest. This book is about brown bears.

Where Brown Bears Live

Brown bears live in forests and mountains in Canada, Alaska, and Russia. A few live in Europe. In North America they are called **grizzly** bears.

Some brown bears live on the cold **Arctic tundra**. There are no trees there and food is hard to find. The bears in this book live in Alaska.

Males and Females

Brown bears like to live on their own. This big male stands up to see if there are any other bears nearby. He will scare them away. Look at his sharp claws.

Female bears live on their own, except when they have **cubs**. This female will look after her cubs for two to four years.

Mating

In the early summer, the male bear travels a long way to find a **mate**. If he meets another male bear, they will fight. Male bears are very fierce.

At last, the male finds a female. He stays
with her for a week or two. After they
have **mated**, he will leave her.

Finding Food

The bears spend many hours looking for food. They eat a lot of grass and berries. They dig the ground with their sharp claws to find insects and small **mammals**.

Bears have very good senses of smell and good memories. This **cub** sniffs some tasty food. She will remember this feeding place. She may come back to it.

Fishing

Brown bears in Canada and Alaska are huge and eat a lot of fish. This **grizzly** is trying to catch a **salmon**. He leans forward hungrily.

Many other bears have arrived. There is
plenty of food for everyone. The bears are
so busy fishing, there is no time to fight.

Winter is Coming

It is fall. Soon snow will cover the plants and there will be no insects. The bears eat as much as they can and grow fat. They will eat nothing all winter.

During the long winter months, the bears sleep in **dens**. They make a hole under rocks or trees. This female will sleep in her den for about six months.

Babies

The **cubs** are born in the winter. Here they are ten days old. Their eyes are still closed. They drink their mother's milk and keep warm in her fur.

In spring the mother and her cubs leave
the **den**. The snow begins to melt. This
cub is three months old and he loves to play.

Growing Up

The **cubs** learn fast. They watch their
mother catch a fish. They already know
how to sniff the ground to find insects
and roots.

This young bear is now two. He still travels with his mother and sister. He knows to watch for danger. In about a year's time, he will go to live on his own.

Brown Bear Facts

- Bears mainly eat plants. They also catch small **mammals** such as ground squirrels and rabbits. Sometimes they hunt young deer too.

- Bears usually give birth to two to four **cubs** at a time, but two cubs is the most common.

- Brown bears can live for 25 years.

- Bears rub their backs against trees to leave their smell. This warns other bears that they are nearby.

- Brown bears can run very fast. Some can run up to 30 miles an hour.

- A bear's claws are 4 inches long. That's probably longer than twice the length of your longest finger!

Glossary

Arctic   Cold, northern part of the world.

cub   Baby bear.

den   Safe, warm hole in the ground.

grizzly   What brown bears are called in Canada and the western United States.

mammal   Animal with hair that feeds its babies on milk.

mate   Partner to have babies with.

mating   Two animals making a baby together.

salmon   Type of large fish.

tundra   Land in the Arctic that is covered by low-growing plants, and where the soil is frozen most of the year.

Index

More Books To Read

Bailey, Donna. *Bears*. Austin, Tex.: Raintree Steck-Vaughn, 1990.

Bour, Laura. *Bears*. New York: Scholastic, 1992.

Fowler, Allan. *Please Don't Feed the Bears*. Chicago: Childrens Press, 1991.